OCS Study MMS 2005-060

FINAL REPORT

Breeding Biology of King Eiders on the Coastal Plain of Northern Alaska

Principal Investigator:

Abby N. Powell
Research Associate Professor, Wildlife Biology
Institute of Arctic Biology
University of Alaska Fairbanks
and Research Wildlife Biologist, USGS
Alaska Cooperative Fish and Wildlife Research Unit

Co-principal Investigator:

Robert Suydam
Wildlife Biologist
North Slope Borough, Barrow, AK

Co-principal Investigator:

Rebecca L. McGuire
Graduate Research Assistant
Department of Biology and Wildlife
University of Alaska Fairbanks

Prepared by:

Rebecca L. McGuire

December 2005

Table of Contents

List of Tables

List of Figures

Abstract

Little is known about the breeding biology of King Eiders (*Somateria spectabilis*), partly because they typically nest in remote areas, in low densities. The western North American population of King Eiders declined by more than 50% between 1976 and 1996 for unknown reasons (Suydam et al. 2000). Additionally, the National Petroleum Reserve-Alaska (NPR-A) is being leased for oil and gas exploration and may potentially be developed. The highest known density of nesting King Eiders on the north slope of Alaska is within the northeast planning areas of NPR-A (Larned et al. 2003). During the summers of 2002 and 2003, we studied King Eiders in an area to the southeast of Teshekpuk Lake within the NPR-A, and in the Kuparuk oilfields on the North Slope of Alaska to provide information on their basic breeding biology and habitat use. We compared timing of nesting, nest success, and habitat use between a relatively undisturbed site at Teshekpuk Lake and the active Kuparuk oilfield.

We found and monitored 39 to 44 active nests each year at each site. King Eiders at both sites selected nests in moist habitats, relatively close to water. Often these nests occurred on islands in tundra thaw lakes. Eiders also experienced higher nest success on these islands, probably due to decreased mammalian predation pressure. We determined that nest success was very low at both sites; this is not surprising for a long-lived, large-bodied species, and is not a cause for concern in itself. Brood survival was also low and females with broods left the breeding areas fairly soon after hatch. However, our sample size for brood survival was low. This study provided critical baseline data on nest success and habitat associations of King Eiders nesting on Alaska's North Slope.

Introduction

King Eiders (*Somateria spectabilis*) are one of the most northerly nesting ducks; seldom nesting below 65° N latitude (Lamothe 1973). Little is known about the breeding biology of King Eiders in either disturbed or undisturbed areas, partly because they typically nest in remote areas, at low densities. To date, there have been few studies dedicated to the breeding biology of King Eiders (Lamothe 1973, Cotter et al. 1997, Kellett and Alisauskas 2000, Kellett 1999, and Kellett and Alisauskas 1997), and most of the knowledge has been anecdotal data collected incidentally to other studies (Suydam 2000). Migration counts at Point Barrow, Alaska have indicated that the western North American population of King Eiders has declined by more than 50% between 1976 and 1996 (Suydam et al. 2000). Similarly, surveys of the western Canadian breeding population have shown a reduction in breeding pairs (Dickson et al. 1997) and Gratto-Trevor et al. (1998) reported an 86% decrease between 1975 and 1995 in the number of King Eiders nesting in the Rasmussen lowlands, NWT. Reasons for the decline are unknown, but it corresponds with continent-wide declines in other sea duck species (Sea Duck Joint Venture 2001). These trends have created an increasing interest in the ecology of King Eiders. Additionally, the highest known density of nesting King Eiders on the north slope of Alaska occurs within the northeast planning area of the National Petroleum Reserve-Alaska (NPR-A). The NPR-A is being leased for oil and gas exploration and is just beginning to be developed.

We examined the factors that influence nest site choice in King Eiders and how nest success is affected by these choices. We investigated nest site selection by comparing nest site characteristics of nests and random points within the same study areas. We modeled nest success to determine the importance of habitat and social factors around the nest site. We examined and compared variation in nest success and nest site choice between a relatively undisturbed site at Teshekpuk Lake and the active oilfield at Kuparuk.

Objectives

- Document the timing of arrival and departure from breeding areas of males, females and young.

- Document habitat use during pre-nesting, nesting and brood-rearing and post-nesting;

- Document chronology of nesting, nesting success, causes of nest failure, and if possible, brood survival.

- Compare data collected from above objectives between Teshekpuk Lake and the Kuparuk Oilfields.

- Evaluate habitat selection through the use of vegetation or land cover databases.

Methods

Study areas

We included two main study sites on the North Slope of Alaska; Teshekpuk Lake and the Kuparuk Oil Fields (Fig.1). The Teshekpuk Lake study site (70°25' N, 153°07' W) was 10 km inland from the southeast shore of the lake and had experienced very little human impact; there was no sign of anthropogenic disturbance and no people other than those connected with this project were observed during the course of the study. The Kuparuk study site (70°20' N, 149°45' W) was an area on the Arctic Coastal Plain between the Colville and Kuparuk rivers leased by ConocoPhillips Alaska Inc. and actively being developed for oil production. Both areas were characterized by numerous thaw lakes, ponds and basins. Wetland community types included wet sedge (*Carex* spp.) meadows, moist sedge-dwarf shrub (*Salix* spp.) meadows, and emergent *Carex* spp. and *Arctophila fulva* on the margins of the lakes and ponds (Anderson et al. 1999). Some wetlands at Kuparuk were intersected by roads and/or created with the closure and rehabilitation of gravel pits.

Field methods

At Teshekpuk, in both years, all King Eiders observed throughout the season were recorded. Arrival and departure dates of King Eiders were not recorded at Kuparuk due to logistical constraints.

Accessible areas around Teshekpuk Lake and Kuparuk were searched for pre-nesting and nesting King Eiders during the summers of 2002 and 2003. Kuparuk had road access between wetlands while the Teshekpuk site did not, allowing us to search a larger area at Kuparuk (Teshekpuk ~1000 ha; Kuparuk ~1500 ha). We marked nests with a tongue depressor placed one meter from the nest in vegetation so as to be concealed from potential nest predators. We measured length, width and weight of each egg. All eggs were candled in 2003 to estimate stage of development (Weller 1956). Latitude and longitude were recorded for each King Eider nest using a hand-held GPS unit. Habitat type within 50 m of each nest was classified post-hatch as to type using Bergman's classification system (1977). Vegetation types and frequency were recorded within one meter of nests (2002 and 2003) and at random locations (only 2003) within the two study areas. Additionally, we recorded island size, distance to the mainland and depth of the water if the nest occurred on an island.

King Eiders typically incubate for 22–24 days and all nests were monitored weekly during this period. Hatch success was determined by the presence of eggshells with detached membranes (Girard 1939) or the presence of ducklings. If there were eggshells with no membranes or if the entire egg was absent, the nest was considered depredated. We attempted to determine cause of failure for nests that did not succeed. Incubation stage (days) was determined from information on egg laying and from candling. We calculated nest initiation dates by subtracting the estimated age of embryos, as determined by candling, plus the number of eggs laid into the nest from the date of discovery (Grand and Flint 1997).

To determine brood survival, we captured females on nests about one week prior to hatch using hand-carried mist nets or bow-net traps. Originally we planned to trap twenty females randomly selected each year for trapping; however, very low nest success of hens required that we attempted to trap any female still on a nest one week prior to predicted hatch date. In 2002, we captured twelve females at Kuparuk and one female at Teshekpuk. Feathers on the upper back between the wings were clipped and 8-g VHF transmitters were attached to the area using epoxy. Due to transmitter loss in 2002, 10-g VHF transmitters were attached to females using an anchor and suture technique in 2003 (Pietz et al. 1995). We captured and fitted twelve hens with transmitters in 2003 at Kuparuk and eight at Teshekpuk. We took morphometric measurements on all hens and each bird was fitted with a USFWS leg band. All transmitters were designed to fall off before fall migration. All methods and handling of birds were approved by the University of Alaska Institutional Animal Care and Use Committee (IACUC # 02-10).

Radio-transmittered hens were tracked by vehicle, foot and air at Kuparuk and on foot at Teshekpuk. After hatch, hens were located every two to five days until chicks were 30 days old or the female was observed twice without a brood. Aerial telemetry flights were flown weekly at Kuparuk, when weather permitted to locate hens not found from the ground. Location information was recorded using GPS and aerial photos. We also recorded number of ducklings in the brood, number of hens and ducklings if broods had amalgamated, general behavior, general habitat description (Bergman et al. 1977) and any predators observed in vicinity.

Data Analysis

Habitat Use

The Teshekpuk study area was contained within the National Petroleum Reserve-Alaska Landcover Inventory database of the Bureau of Land Management and Ducks Unlimited. In this database, vegetation types were classified as follows: clear water, turbid water, ice, *Carex aquatilis, Arctophila fulva*, flooded tundra-low centered polygons, flooded tundra-non-pattern, wet tundra, sedge/grass meadow, tussock tundra, moss/lichen, dwarf shrub, low shrub, tall shrub, dunes/dry sand, sparsely vegetated, barren ground/other (see appendix for details). Random locations within the study area were generated using an ArcView extension, Random Point Generator. Distances to the perimeter of the nearest lake from King Eider nests and the random locations were calculated using the spatial join option of the extension Geoprocessing Wizard. The large cell size (30 m) made some habitat analyses difficult as nests on small islands appeared to be in the water. However, vegetation type within 30 m of a nest could be compared to random sites and to the study area as a whole. Here we report on vegetation class availability and use within the Teshekpuk study area in 2002. Analyses were conducted in ArcView GIS 3.3.

Nest Site Selection

Nest site selection was examined by comparing the characteristics of nests and random points using logistic regression analyses at two scales, 1 m and 50 m, at both sites in 2003. Random locations within the study area were generated using an ArcView extension, Random Point Generator, visited on foot, and habitat variables were recorded (see field methods). At the 50 m scale we included the following explanatory variables: presence/absence of low polygons, low-centered polygons, high-centered polygons, peninsulas, troughs, strangmoors, and meadows within 50 m of the nest or random location; length of the closest water body, distance to the closest water body, mainland/island location, distance to nearest Glaucous Gull (*Larus hyperboreus*) nest and distance to the nearest King Eider nest. We

used logistic regression analysis and Akaike's Information Criterion values adjusted for a small sample size (AIC_c) to select the best model in the candidate model sets. Separate analyses were performed for the two sites. We used model averaging to derive parameter estimates (denoted as $\theta \pm SE$) and 95% confidence limits from a greater than 92% confidence set of candidate models (Burnham and Anderson 2002).

At the 1 m scale we included the variable's distance to water and the percentage of the following vegetation groups within 1 m of the nest or random location: carex, eriophorum, salix, dryas, cassiope, moss, ledum and lichen. As all of the vegetation types were highly correlated with one another, we used principal components analysis to reduce the dimensionality of the data. We attempted to interpret all eigenvalues with a variance > 1. We then used the scores of the interpretable eigenvectors as explanatory variable in a logistic regression analysis. Akaike's Information Criterion values adjusted for a small sample size (AIC_c) were used to select the best model in the candidate model sets at both sites separately. SAS (SAS Institute 1990) was used for all analysis.

Nest survival

We used Program MARK to test for site-, year-, and island/mainland-specific differences in nest survival and to investigate the importance of spatial covariates (distance to the nearest conspecific nest, distance to the nearest larid nest, distance to water, and distance to the mainland), as well as any linear trends in time throughout the season (T) on daily nest survival rates (White and Burnham 1999, Dinsmore et al. 2002). Linear relationships between covariates and daily survival were examined to determine what, if any, effect is present. A link function was used to characterize the relationship between daily nest survival and the covariates. We used the logit link as it is the natural link for the binomial distribution (McCullagh and Nelder 1989). We did not adjust for overdispersion, as no accurate method for estimation exists for small sample sizes (Dinsmore et al. 2002).

Brood rearing

Movements of females were plotted using ArcView GIS (ESRI 1998). Distance between resightings and direction of brood movements were calculated using Animal Movement extension (Hooge and Eichenlaub 1997) in ArcView. We considered survival of a brood as one duckling in a brood surviving to 30 days of age. Amalgamation of broods was not extensive at either study site. When brood amalgamation was observed, we considered a radio-transmittered hen to still have a brood if ducklings of the appropriate age tended to follow her when disturbed rather than alternate hens. Linear regression was used to test whether the number of days a brood survived was affected by distances traveled each day at Kuparuk (small sample size at Teshekpuk precluded analysis). Means are presented ± SE. Data from both years are combined in all analyses, due to small sample sizes. All statistical analyses were performed using SAS software (SAS Institute 1990).

Results

Upon our arrival at the Teshekpuk study site (7 June 2002, 11 June 2003), King Eiders were present in an equal ratio of males to females. The sex ratio continued to be about equal until after 19 June in 2002 and slightly later (25 June) in 2003, when males began to depart the study area. No males were seen in the study area after 28 June 2002 and 8 July 2003 (Fig. 2). We found and monitored 39 – 44 active nests each year at each site. Initiation of incubation in 2003 ranged from 5 – 30 June at Kuparuk with most females beginning incubation around 25 June. Initiation ranged from 11 June to 4 July with most females beginning incubation around 23 June at Teshekpuk in 2003 (Fig. 3). Nest initiation was not different between Kuparuk and Teshekpuk in 2003 (t = -0.75, $P < 0.46$). Most nests were found during laying at both sites in 2003 and more than 60% of nests were found in the first week of incubation (Fig. 4).

Habitat Use

Based on the landcover database, the percent covers of the dominant vegetation types within the study area were as follows: clear water (14%), turbid water (17%), *Carex aquatilis* (10%), sedge meadow (23%), and tussock tundra (14%) (Fig. 5). However, there were numerous small islands in some of these lakes that did not show up on the landcover map because they were smaller than the cell size of 30 m.

Forty seven King Eider nests were located in a variety of habitat types during nest searches at Teshekpuk in 2002. The distribution of nests throughout the study area appeared to be clumped with nests occurring in and around lakes. Analysis of the vegetation type of the landcover gridcell that each King Eider nest was located in indicated that nests occurred most often in turbid water (40%), followed by clear water (28%; Fig. 5). These nests were not in the water, as it would seem from the database, but on islands with the dominant habitat type within 30 m being either clear or turbid water. The flooded tundra low-center polygon vegetation type was also used more frequently (12%) than it occurred within the study site. However, this

was a much smaller difference in availability and use than seen for clear and turbid water.

King Eider nests occurred 24.4 ± 0.97 (m, SE) from the shoreline of either clear or turbid lakes. Random locations throughout the study area fell 81.2 ± 2.1 (m, SE) from lakes. Nests and random points that fell within the borders of a lake were assigned the distance of zero to the border of that lake. Eider nests were located primarily on islands (70.8%) but peninsulas and other landforms were also used. Nests that appeared to be within the boundaries of lakes (on islands) were 60.4 ± 1.2 (m, SE) from the shore.

Nest Site Selection

Teshekpuk – The logistic regression model at the 50 m scale for Teshekpuk in 2003 that best discriminated between occupied and unoccupied nest sites included island/mainland location, presence of a low polygon within 50 m, length of the closest waterbody and distance to nearest conspecific (Table 1). There are four candidate models within 2 AIC_c values from the best approximating model, all of which included the variables in the top model. A Hosmer-Lemeshow Goodness-of-Fit ($\chi^2 = 8.86$, $P = 0.26$) test indicated a good fit of the data to the logistic model. Nest sites were more likely to be on islands near larger lakes, and unlikely to be found near other eider or low polygons (Table 2). However, none of these model-averaged parameter estimates were significant.

Principle components analysis of the vegetation types within 1 m of the nest site revealed five eigenvalues with a variance greater than one. We interpreted the factor loadings as the following habitat types; dry tussock tundra dominated by eriophorum, lichen and forbs (tussock), moist tundra dominated by cassiope (moist), dry tundra dominated by cassiope and dryas (dry), dry tundra dominated by salix and carex (dry salix), and moist tundra dominated by salix (moist salix; Table 3). The logistic regression model that best described nest sites at the 1 m scale included the habitat types: tussock, moist, dry salix, and moist salix (Table 4). The best approximating model was 2.29 AIC_c units from the next best model indicating high support for the top model. A Hosmer-Lemeshow Goodness-of-Fit ($\chi^2 = 5.13$, $P = 0.74$) test indicated a good fit of the data to the logistic model. King Eiders tended to select nest sites in moist tundra or moist salix dominated tundra and to avoid tussock tundra dominated sites (Table 5).

Kuparuk – Nest site choice of King Eiders at Kuparuk in 2003 revealed a slightly different pattern from Teshekpuk. The logistic regression model at the 50 m scale that best discriminated between occupied and unoccupied nest sites included presence of high center polygons, troughs and peninsulas within 50 m, and distance to water, conspecifics and Glaucous Gulls (Table 6). There are an additional four models within 2 AIC_c values from the top model causing model selection uncertainty. However, the variables in the top model appear in 4 of 5 top models. A Hosmer-Lemeshow Goodness-of-Fit ($\chi^2 = 1.97$, $P = 0.96$) test indicated a good fit of the data to the logistic model. Nest sites were more likely to be found near conspecific nests, Glaucous Gulls, peninsulas and on islands; and were unlikely to be found very close to water, troughs or high center polygons (Table 7). However, only the model-averaged parameter estimate of trough was significant.

Principle components analysis of the vegetation types within 1 m of the nest site revealed five eigenvalues with a variance greater than one. We interpreted the factor loadings as the following habitat types; dry tundra dominated by ledum and lichen (dry), dry tundra dominated by salix and moss (dry salix), moist tundra dominated by salix and dryas (moist salix), moist tundra dominated by carex (carex meadow), and moist forb dominated tundra (moist forb; Table 8). Some of the habitat classifications were similar to those at Teshekpuk, and have the same titles; however, factor loadings do not exactly correspond between the two sites. The logistic regression model that best described nest sites at the one meter scale included dry, dry salix, moist salix, and carex meadow vegetation classifications (Table 9). The top model is only 0.29 AIC values from the next best model, which does not have an effect of dry salix. A Hosmer-

Lemeshow Goodness-of-Fit ($\chi^2 = 7.9$, $P = 0.34$) test indicated a good fit of the data to the logistic model. King Eiders at Kuparuk in 2003 tended to avoid choosing sites in dry, dry salix and in the moist salix dominated tundra, and select carex meadow tundra (Table 10). However, only the model-averaged parameter estimate of the dry vegetation classification was significant.

Nest success

The daily survival of King Eider nests was a function of both the island vs. mainland nest location, and the site, Teshekpuk vs. Kuparuk (Table 11). Nests on islands had significantly higher daily survival than those on the mainland (Table 12). The estimate from the best model for the additive effect on survival of nests on islands compared to those on the mainland was $\beta_{island} = 0.66$ (1 SE = 0.21, 95% CL = 0.26, 1.06) on a logit scale and this coefficient was always positive in models with island effects. Models incorporating site received substantial support; Kuparuk was always slightly higher than Teshekpuk, but not significantly so. Models with linear trends on nest survival received some support; quadratic trends received slightly less support. The confidence intervals for the coefficients of both the linear and quadratic trends included zero. Daily nest survival increased throughout the season at Teshekpuk $B_{T(Teshekpuk)} = 0.02$ (1 SE = 0.02, 95% CL = -0.03, 0.06) and decreased at Kuparuk $B_{T(Kuparuk)} = -0.02$ (1 SE = 0.02, 95% CL = -0.06, 0.02; Fig.6). There was no evidence of year effects on nest survival. There was some support for an effect of distance to the nearest other King Eider nest $\beta_{conspecifc\ at\ Kuparuk} = 0.12$ (1 SE = 0.13, 95% CL = -0.13, 0.37), and $\beta_{conspecific\ at\ Teshekpuk} = -0.09$ (1 SE = 0.21, 95% CL = -0.50, 0.33). However, confidence intervals for the coefficients included zero for both Teshekpuk (survival decreased as conspecific distance increased) and Kuparuk (survival increased with conspecific distance), and thus the estimated effect was slight. Most nest failure was due to depredation and usually all the eggs were gone; there were no shells left in the nest, and no tracks. Since we observed foxes, Glaucous Gulls and Common Ravens (*Corvus corax*) transporting entire eggs it is impossible to determine with any certainty which nest predators were responsible.

Brood rearing

Teshekpuk – Unfortunately, tracking brood movements at Teshekpuk was not successful in 2002. The one female that was transmittered successfully hatched but left the study area immediately and we were unable to follow her due to our inability to efficiently track on foot; bad weather precluded aerial tracking. Eight hens were trapped at Teshekpuk in 2003. Of these hens, only three successfully hatched eggs. Two of the hens with broods were followed for over a week before they traveled too far away to be located on foot. Both broods remained in marshes within 1 km of their nest site for approximately one week. One brood appeared to be heading north before we could no longer find it, while the other did not have a clear direction of movement. Both of these hens still had chicks when they where last located. We failed to locate the third female and her brood after hatch. No broods were relocated at 30 days of age or greater.

Kuparuk – Of the hens captured in 2002, five were successfully radio-tracked with broods at Kuparuk. Of the hens transmittered in 2002 that were not tracked, four failed to successfully hatch eggs and three prematurely dropped their radio transmitters. In 2003, six hens were successfully tracked. Of the hens transmittered in 2003 that were not radio-tracked, three failed prior to hatch and three lost broods prior to first relocation after hatch. Apparent brood survival to 30 days of age was 20% (n = 10). Broods survived 13.4 ± 3.1 days (n = 10) on average. Mean daily movement rates of hens with broods were 470 ± 61.7 m/day (n = 10, range 178.3 – 826.9 m). Longer daily movement rates did not affect the number of days a brood survived ($F = 1.51$, $P = 0.25$).

Two radioed hens with broods were observed in crèches. These hens were the only two that successfully raised young to 30 days. One hen hatched five ducklings, but was later observed with three King Eider and three Spectacled Eider (*Somateria fischeri*) chicks. Ultimately this hen was observed in a crèche of up to 40 hens and 12 young. We believe some of these ducklings were still associated with the radioed hen based on behavioral observations. When the crèche was disturbed, we observed that hens still associated with broods would split from the larger group and move toward shore with young. The second hen that successfully raised two ducklings to 30 days formed a small crèche with one other hen with a brood of two chicks. The two broods were discernable by their different size, with our hen having smaller, younger ducklings than the hen with which she formed a crèche.

Discussion

Timing

Males departed the study areas as females began incubation and were not usually seen in July. The time of departure of males varied slightly between years, this is likely correlated with initiation of incubation and spring conditions. We observed groups of females without ducklings in mid- to late-July. Presumably these were failed nesters that group up prior to leaving the breeding areas. We were unable to adequately document the timing of departure from the breeding sites for females with young. However, the few females that we followed at Teshekpuk appeared to leave the study area very quickly after hatch. Kuparuk females experienced low brood survival but survival was not correlated with distance moved per day. It is unknown where the broods moved, what habitats they used, and what factors effected duckling survival, especially at Teshekpuk. These questions are very important in the face of future development on the North Slope of Alaska. However, given the extremely low nest success of King Eider, it will be difficult to ever obtain an adequate sample size for brood survival analysis or habitat selection analysis. Possibly aerial surveys could identify important brood rearing lakes.

Habitat Use

Ducks Unlimited Inc. (1998) found that King Eiders select most strongly for *Carex aquatilis* and *Arctophila fulva* while avoiding ice, tussock tundra, dwarf shrub, dry sand, sparsely vegetated and barren ground habitat types within the NPR-A. The Ducks Unlimited study used the same land cover database that was used in the present study. Within the study area southeast of Teshekpuk, King Eiders selected most strongly for the islands in clear and turbid water. This may be due to nest predator avoidance, as foxes are the main predator in the area and are probably somewhat deterred by having to swim out to a nest. King Eiders did not select strongly for *Arctophila fulva* as was seen in the Ducks Unlimited study, however, very little of this land cover class actually occurred in this area. King Eiders also did not select for *Carex aquatilis*, using it less often than it occurred in the study area. There may be several explanations for this divergence from Ducks Unlimited's results. One difference was the scale; they examined the entire NPR-A, relying on aerial surveys, while we concentrated on a smaller area, covering it on foot. The results from our study do offer further support that the King Eiders are not selecting tussock tundra. We cannot look at the preference or avoidance of some of the other land cover classes because of their low occurrence within the study area. Additionally, we used nest sites that we knew the location of with certainty; Ducks Unlimited used locations of pairs located during aerial surveys. Pairs may flush away from an oncoming aircraft and the location recorded may not be the area they originally selected. Pairs have been observed resting and feeding in areas that are some distance from the actual nest site, causing an estimation of breeding pair habitat selection, not nest site choice.

King Eider nests on islands within lakes were found to be closer to the shore than random locations within lakes in the study area. This may have more to do with the distribution of the islands within the lakes than to the selection of islands by eiders. The method of generating random locations within the lakes did not take into consideration whether an island actually occurred under them or not. This is because most islands cannot be detected at this pixel size. For this same reason we could not compare vegetation classes between the islands that the King Eiders selected and those that they did not. This is a shortfall of the landcover data base and one that should be addressed in future studies.

Nest site selection and nest success

King Eiders at Teshekpuk selected nest sites on islands in or near larger lakes, away from other nesting King Eiders, and avoided low polygons. However, individual model-averaged parameter estimates were largely insignificant. At the microhabitat level eiders selected nest sites in moist tundra or moist salix-dominated tundra and to avoid tussock-tundra dominated sites. King Eiders at Teshekpuk had higher nest success on islands. This was likely due to fewer nesting on an island and would not confer any protection from avian predators.

King Eider nest sites at Kuparuk were more likely to be found near conspecific nests, Glaucous Gulls, peninsulas and on islands; and were unlikely to be found very close to water, troughs or high center polygons (Table 7). However, only the model-averaged parameter estimate of trough was significant. Troughs are largely associated with drier areas dominated by high center polygons (pers obs) and it is likely that eiders are not so much avoiding troughs as selecting areas that do not have troughs, i.e. complex (islands and peninsulas) wetland basins. At the microhabitat scale, King Eiders at Kuparuk avoided choosing sites in the dry vegetation classification. Again, this is an indication that they choose areas away from the dry troughs and high center polygons. Similarly,

nests on islands at Kuparuk experienced higher success.

We were unable to determine causes of nest failure from sign at depredated nests. We recommend that future work further investigate the causes of nest failure and determine if mammalian or avian predators are having a greater effect on nest success. Video systems would likely be the best method to accomplish this, given the problems plaguing motion-triggered camera systems and physical clues left at nest sites. It has been suggested that an effect of development is increased densities of predators in the oilfields. These predators prey on the eggs, nestlings and fledglings of many birds, including King Eiders (Lamothe 1973, Larson 1960, and Kellett and Alisauskas 1997). In order to manage and mitigate the effects of oil development it is very important that we understand factors influencing nest success.

Summary

Prior to this study, there was little known about King Eider breeding biology (Kellett and Alisauskas 1997, Kellett 1999, Lamothe 1973) and what was known was from a semi-colonial island nesting population in arctic Canada (Kellett and Alisauskas 1997, Kellett 1999). In what is likely a more typical scenario across the breeding range of King Eider, we found King Eiders nesting dispersed and solitary on very small islands in tundra thaw lakes, and near the margins of these lakes. King Eiders often nested on islands, probably to avoid nest predators. We found that King Eider selected sites where the microhabitat was moist (close to water), potentially for predator avoidance or easy access to food sources. We determined that nest success was low at both study sites; this was not surprising for a long-lived, large-bodied species. Brood survival was also low and females with broods left the breeding areas fairly soon after hatch. At this point we do not know where King Eider broods go during the brood rearing period, and this knowledge could be important to mitigate and minimize any impacts of oil extraction on the North Slope of Alaska.

We cannot make direct implications of any effect of oil development with this study because we included only one developed and one undisturbed site. The differences we found could be an effect of distance to coast, habitat quality, size of wetlands, or a number of other factors including anthropogenic disturbance. Regardless, we feel that these data were critical for a baseline understanding of the nesting ecology of King Eider. Additionally, our study provided an excellent baseline data set if development proceeds in the Teshekpuk area.

Acknowledgements

This study would not be possible without the financial and logistical support of Coastal Marine Institute, Minerals Management Service, ConocoPhillips Alaska, Inc., University of Alaska Foundation Angus Gavin Grant, USGS Alaska Cooperative Fish and Wildlife Research Unit, and the North Slope Borough. This study was endorsed by the Sea Duck Joint Venture. We thank Chuck Monnett, Jeff Gleason, Doloros Vinas, Liza DelaRosa, April Brower, Benny Akootchook, Justin Harth, and Anne Lazenby for logistical help; Yumiko Uchiro, Kim Hanish, Qiayaan Opie, Bonnie Rogers, Lori Gildehaus, and Rita Frantz for their help as field technicians; and ABR for cooperation at Kuparuk. We also thank Jeff Gleason and two anonymous for their comments on this report.

Study products

Presentations:

McGuire, R. and A. Powell. 2005. Incubation behavior of king eiders on the North Slope of Alaska. Annual Meeting, Pacific Seabird Group/Waterbird Society Meeting, 19–23 January, Portland, OR.

McGuire, R., A. Powell, and R. Suydam. 2005. Breeding biology and habitat use of king eiders on the coastal plain of northern Alaska. 10th Annual MMS Information Transfer Meeting, Anchorage, AK.

McGuire, R. L., R. Suydam, and A. N. Powell. 2005. Breeding biology and habitat use of king eider on the coastal plain of northern Alaska. CMI Annual Research Review, University of Alaska, Fairbanks, AK.

McGuire, R. L., L. Phillips, R. Suydam, and A. N. Powell. 2004. Breeding biology and habitat use by king eider (*Somateria spectabilis*) at Teshekpuk Lake and Kuparuk oilfields on the North Slope of Alaska. CMI Annual Research Review, University of Alaska, Fairbanks, AK.

McGuire, R., L. Phillips, A. N. Powell, and R. Suydam. 2004. Factors influencing king eider nest survival on Alaska's North Slope. 16 March 2004, Alaska Bird Conference, Anchorage, AK.

Knoche, M., R. McGuire, L. Phillips, and H. Wilson. 2004. Alaska's eiders. Presentation at Alaska Bird Observatory's seminar series.

McGuire, R. L., L. Phillips, R. Suydam, and A. N. Powell. 2004. Breeding biology and habitat use of king eiders on the coastal plain of northern Alaska.

McGuire, R. L., L. Phillips, R. Suydam, and A. N. Powell. 2003. Breeding biology and habitat use by king eider (*Somateria spectabilis*) at Teshekpuk Lake and Kuparuk oilfields on the North Slope of Alaska. CMI Annual Research Review, University of Alaska, Fairbanks, AK.

McGuire, R. L., L. Phillips, R. Suydam, and A. N. Powell. 2002. Breeding biology and habitat use by king eider at Teshekpuk Lake and Kuparuk oil fields on the north slope of Alaska. Poster; North American Sea Duck Conference, 6–10 November 2002, Victoria, B.C.

Powell, A. N. 2002. Ecology of king eiders on Alaska's North Slope. Oral paper presented at the MMS Information Transfer Seminar, Anchorage, AK.

Reports:

Powell, A. N., R. Suydam, and R. McGuire. 2004. Breeding Biology of King Eiders on the Coastal Plain of Northern Alaska. Annual Report, CMI, University of Alaska, Fairbanks.

Powell, A. N., R. Suydam, R. McGuire, and L. Phillips. 2004. Breeding biology and habitat use of King Eiders on the Coastal Plain of Northern Alaska. Report to the Sea Duck Joint Venture, Endorsed Study No. 25.
http://www.seaduckjv.org/ssna.html

Powell, A. N., R. Suydam, and R. McGuire. 2003. Breeding Biology of King Eiders on the Coastal Plain of Northern Alaska. Annual Report, CMI, University of Alaska, Fairbanks.

Powell, A. N., R. Suydam, R. McGuire, and L. Phillips. 2003. Breeding biology and habitat use of King Eiders on the Coastal Plain of Northern Alaska. Report to the Sea Duck Joint Venture, Endorsed Study No. 25.
http://www.seaduckjv.org/ssna.html

Powell, A. N., R. Suydam, and R. McGuire. 2002. Breeding Biology of King Eiders on the Coastal Plain of Northern Alaska. Annual Report, CMI, University of Alaska, Fairbanks.

Literature Cited

Anderson B. A., C. B. Johnson, B. A. Cooper, L. N. Smith, and A. A. Stickney. 1999. Habitat associations of nesting spectacled eiders on the Arctic Coastal Plain of Alaska. *Pp.* 27–32 *In:* R. I. Goudie, M. R. Peterson, G. J. Robertson (ed.) Behavior and ecology of sea ducks. Can Wildl. Ser. Occasional. Paper 100. 87pp.

Bergman, R. D., R. L. Howard, K. F. Abraham, and M. F. Weller. 1977. Water birds and their wetland resources in relation to oil development at Storkersen Point, Alaska. U.S. Fish and Wildl. Serv. Resour. Publ. 29, Washington D.C. 38pp.

Burgess, R. M., J. R. Rose, P. W. Banyas, and B. E. Lawhead. 1993. Arctic fox studies in the Prudhoe Bay Unit and adjacent undeveloped areas, 1992. Prepared by Alaska Biological Research, Inc., Fairbanks, AK. for BP exploration (Alaska) Inc., Anchorage, Ak.

Burnham, K. P., and D. R. Anderson. 2002. Model selection and Multimodel Inference: A Practical Information-Theoretic Approach, 2nd ed. Springer-Werlag, New York.

Cotter, R. C., D. L. Dickson, and C. J. Gratto.1997. Breeding biology of the King Eider in the western Canadian Arctic. Pages 29–39. *In:* Occasional Paper Number 94. Canadian Wildlife Service.

Dickson, D. L., R. C. Cotter, J. E. Hines, and M. F. Kay. 1997. Distribution and abundance of king eiders in the western Canadian Arctic. *In:* Dickson D. L., editor, King and common eiders of the western Canadian Arctic. Ottawa, Canada: Can. Wildl. Serv. p 29–39.

Dinsmore, S. J., G. C. White, and F. L. Knopf. 2002. Advanced techniques for modeling avian nest survival. Ecology 83:3476–3488.

Ducks Unlimited Inc. 1998. Waterfowl earth cover selection analysis within the National Petroleum Reserve-Alaska. Prepared by Ducks Unlimited Inc., Rancho Cordova, California for U.S. Department of the Interior, Anchorage Alaska.

Eberhardt, L. E., W. C. Hanson, J. L. Bengtson, R. A. Garrott, and E. E. Hanson. 1982. Arctic fox home range characteristics in an oil development area. Can. Field. Nat. 97:66–70.

Girard, G. L. 1939. Notes on the life history of the shoveler. Trans. North Am. Wildl. Conf. 4:364–371.

Grand, J. B., and P. L. Flint. 1999. Productivity of nesting Spectacled Eiders on the Lower Kashunak River, Alaska. Condor 99:926–932.

Gratto-Trevor, C. L., V. H. Johnston, and S. T Pepper. 1998. Changes in shorebird and eider abundance in the Rasmussen Lowlands, NWT. Wilson Bull. 110:316–325.

Hooge, P. N., and B. Eichenlaub [online]. 1997. Animal movement extension to ArcView. Ver 1.1. http://www.absc.usgs.gov/glba/gistools/ (January 2005).

Kellett, D. K., and R. T. Alisauskas. 2000. Body-mass dynamics of King Eiders during incubation. Auk 117:812–817.

Kellett, D. K. 1999. Causes and consequences of variation in nest success of King Eiders (*Somateria spectabilis*) at Karrak Lake, Northwest Territories. M.Sc.Thesis, University of Saskatchewan, Saskatoon.

Kellett, D. K., and R. T. Alisauskas. 1997. Breeding biology of King Eiders nesting on Karrak Lake, Northwest Territories. Arctic 50:47–54.

Lamothe, P. 1973. Biology of the King Kider (Somateria spectabilis) in a freshwater breeding area on Bathurst Island, N.W.T. M.Sc. Thesis, University of Alberta, Edmonton, Alberta.

Larned, W., R. Stehn, and R. Platte. 2003. Eider breeding population survey arctic coastal plain, Alaska 2003. U.S. Fish and Wildlife Service.

Larson, S. 1960. On the influence of the arctic fox *Alopex lagopus* on the distribution of arctic birds. Oikos 11:276–305.

McCullagh, P., and J. A. Nelder. 1989. Generalized linear models, 2nd ed. Chapman and Hall, New York.

National Research Council. 2003. Cumulative environmental effects of oil and gas activities on Alaska's north slope. The National Academies Press, Washington, D.C.

Pietz, P. J., D. A. Brandt, G. L. Krapu, and D. A. Buhl. 1995. Modified transmitter attachment method for adult ducks. Journal of Field Ornithology 66:408–417.

SAS Institute. 1990. SAS/STAT User's Guide, version 6, 4th ed. SAS Institute, Cary, North Carolina.

Sea Duck Joint Venture Management Board. 2001. Sea Duck Joint Venture Strategic Plan: 2001–2006. SDJV Continental Technical Team. Unpubl. Rept. [c/o USFWS, Anchorage Alaska; CWS, Sackville, New Brunswick]. 14pp. + appendices.

Suydam, R. S. 2000. King Eider (*Somateria spectabilis*). *In*: The Birds of North America, No. 491. (A. Poole and F. Gill, eds.). The Birds of North America, Inc., Philadelphia, PA.

Suydam, R. S., D. L. Dickson, J. B. Fadely, and L. T. Quakenbush. 2000. Population declines of King and Common Eiders of the Beaufort Sea. Condor 102:219–222.

Truett, J. L., M. E. Miller, and K. Kertell. 1997. Effects of arctic Alaska oil development on brand and snow geese. Arctic 50:138–146.

Weller, J. W. 1956. A simple field candler for waterfowl eggs. Journal of Wildlife Management 20:111–113

White, G. C., and K. P. Burnham. 1999. Program MARK: survival estimation from populations of marked animals. Bird Study 46 Supplement: 120–138.

Appendix

Clear Water – Fresh or saline waters with little or no particulate matter. Clear water areas are typically deep (greater than 1 m). The clear water class may contain small amounts of *Arctophila fulva* or *Carex aquatilis* but generally less than 15% surface coverage of these species.

Turbid Water – Waters that contain particulate matter or shallow (<1m), clear water bodies that are spectrally different from class 1.1. This class typically occurs in shallow lake shelves, deltaic plumes, and rivers and lakes with high sediment loads. The turbid water class may contain small amounts of *Arctophila fulva* or *Carex aquatilis* but generally less than 15% surface coverage of these species.

Ice – May last into late summer on lakes and larger ponds. Ice is present year round in many of the larger lakes.

Carex aquatilis – Associated with lake or pond shorelines and composed of 50 – 80% clear or turbid water that was greater than 10 centimeters deep. The dominant species was *Carex aquatilis*. A small percentage of *Arctophila fulva, Hippuris vulgaris, Potentilla palustris,* and *Caltha palustris* may be present.

Arctophila fulva – Associated with lake or pond shorelines and composed of 50 – 80% clear or turbid water that was greater than 10 centimeters deep. The dominant species was *Arctophila fulva*. A small percentage of *Carex aquatilis, Hippuris vulgaris, Potentilla palustris,* and *Caltha palustris* may also be present.

Flooded Tundra–Low Centered Polygons – Polygon features that retain water throughout the summer. This class is composed of 25 – 50% water; *Carex aquatilis* is the dominant species in the permanently flooded areas. The dryer ridges of the polygons are composed mostly of *Eriophorum russeolum, Eriophorum vaginatum, Sphagnum* spp., *Salix* spp., *Betula nana, Arctostaphylos* spp., and *Ledum palustre*.

Flooded Tundra–Non-pattern – Continuously flooded areas composed of 25 – 50% water. *Carex aquatilis* was the dominant species. Other species may include *Hippuris vulgaris, Potentilla palustris,* and *Caltha palustris*. Non-pattern is distinguished from low centered polygons by the lack of polygon features and associated shrub species that grow on the dry ridges of low centered polygons.

Wet Tundra – Associated with areas of super saturated soils and standing water. Wet tundra often floods in early summer and generally drains of excess water during dry periods but remains saturated throughout the summer. It is composed of 10 – 25% water; *Carex aquatilis* is the dominant species. Other species may include *Eriophorum angustifolium,* and other sedges, grasses, and forbs.

Sedge/Grass Meadow – Dominated by the sedge family. This class commonly consists of a continuous mat of sedges and grasses with a moss and lichen understory. The dominant species were *Carex aquatilis, Eriophorum angustifolium, Eriophorum russeolum, Arctagrostis latifolia* and *Poa arctica*. Associated genera include *Cassiope* spp., *Ledum* spp., and *Vaccinium* spp..

Tussock Tundra – Dominated by the tussock-forming sedge *Eriophorum vaginatum*. Tussock tundra is common throughout the Arctic Foothills and may be found on well-drained sites in all areas of the NPR-A. Cottongrass tussocks are the dominant landscape elements, while moss is the common understory. Lichen, forbs and shrubs are also present in varying densities. Associated genera include *Salix* spp., *Betula nana, Ledum palustre,* and *Carex* spp..

Moss/Lichen – Associated with low lying lakeshores and dry sandy ridges dominated by moss and lichen species. As this type grades into a sedge type, graminoids such as *Carex aquatilis* may increase in cover, forming an intermediate zone.

Dwarf Shrub – Associated with ridges and well drained soils and dominated by shrubs less than 30 centimeters in height. Because of the relative dryness of the sites on which this cover type occurs, it is the most species diverse. Major species included *Salix* spp., *Betula nana, Ledum palustre, Dryas* spp., *Vaccinium* spp., *Arctostaphylos* spp., *Eriophorum vaginatum, and Carex aquatilis*. This class frequently occurs over a substrate of tussocks.

Figures

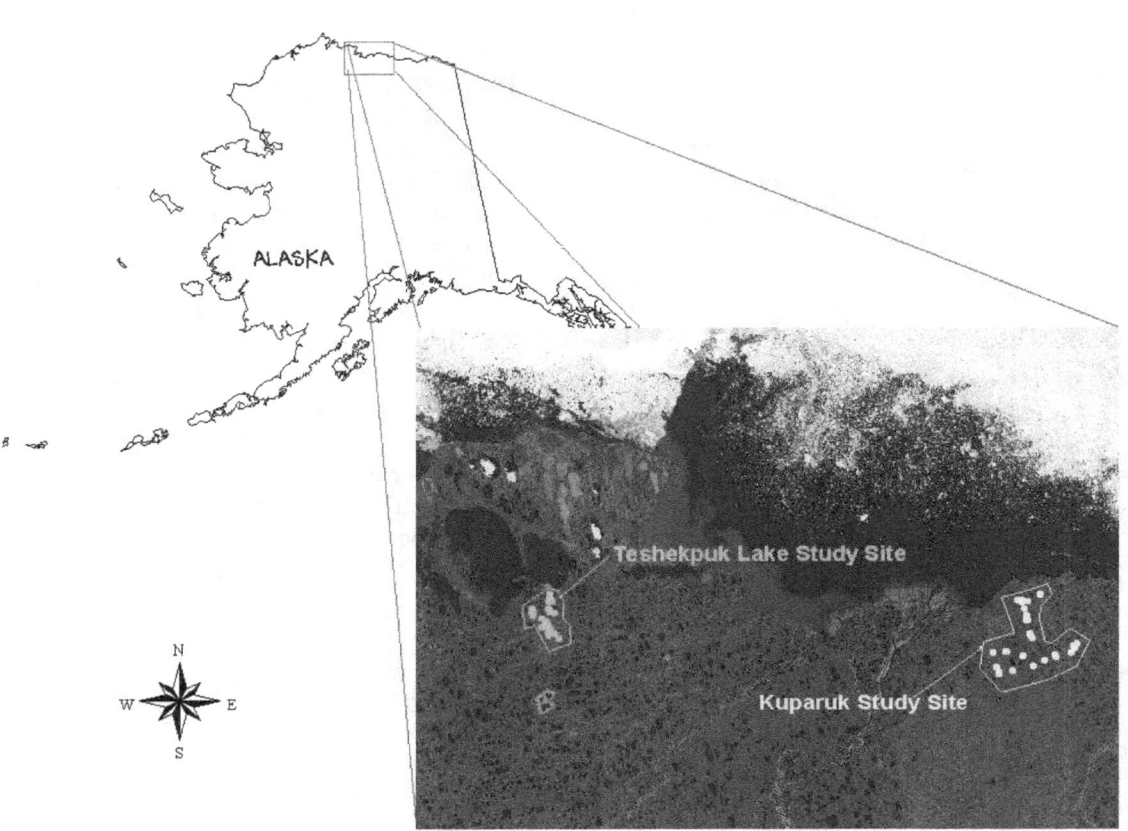

Figure 1. Teshekpuk and Kuparuk study areas on the coastal plain of northern Alaska. King Eider nest locations in 2002 are indicated in green and yellow.

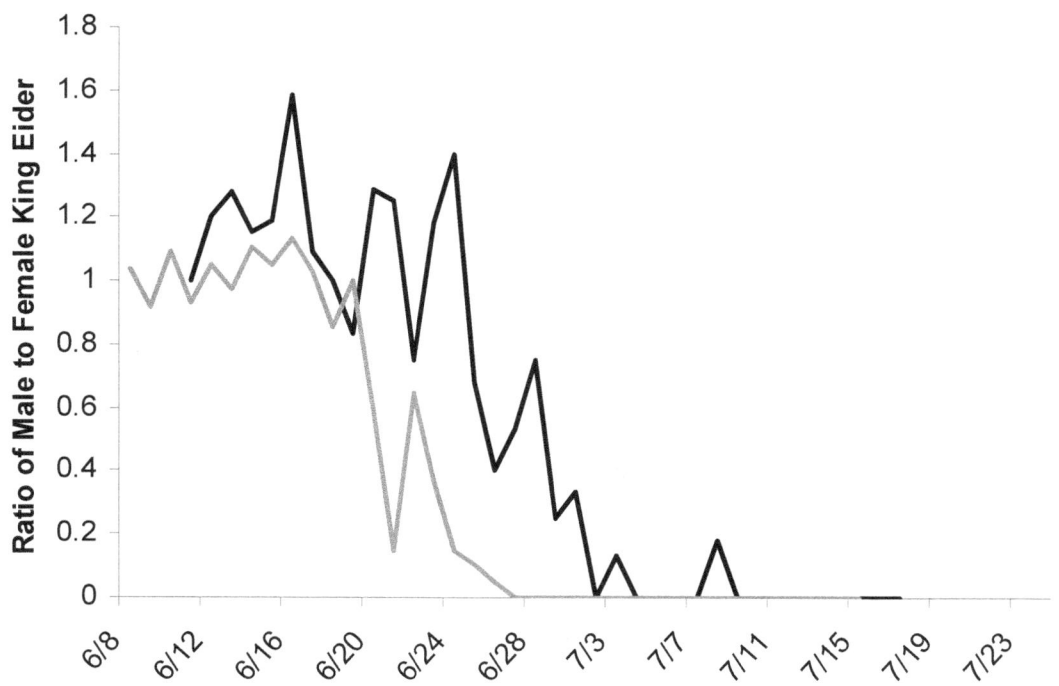

Figure 2. The change in sex ratios of King Eiders observed at Teshekpuk Lake in June and July 2002 (grey line, n = 1589) and 2003 (black line, n = 832).

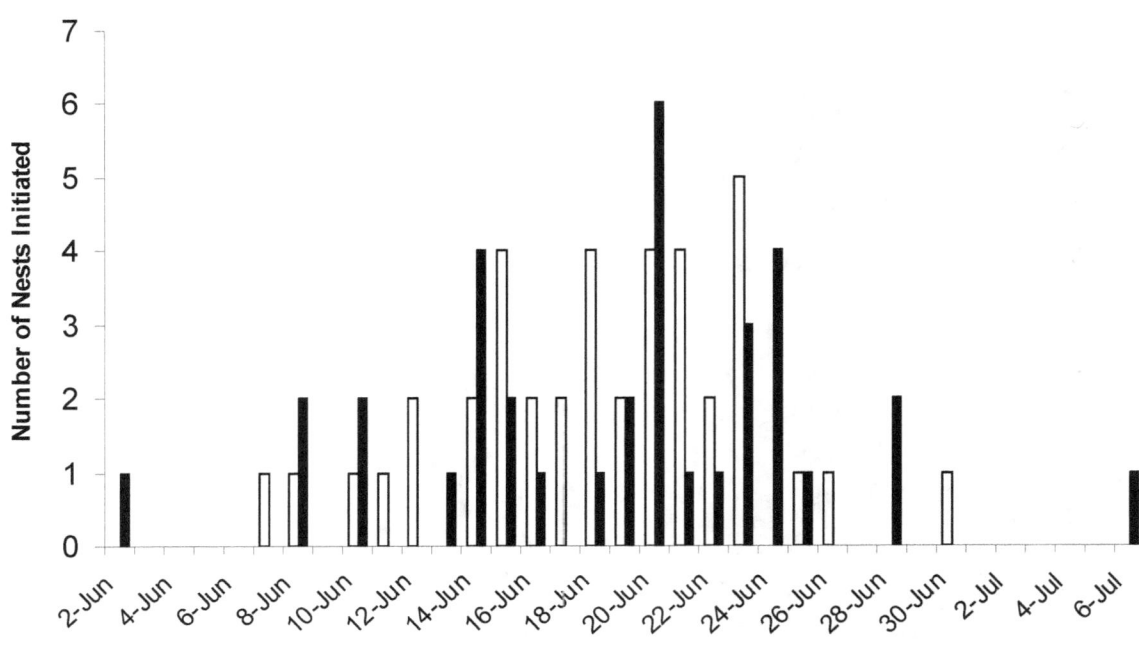

Figure 3. Initiation of egg-laying for King Eider females at Teshekpuk (white, n = 40) and Kuparuk (black, n = 39), Alaska, 2003.

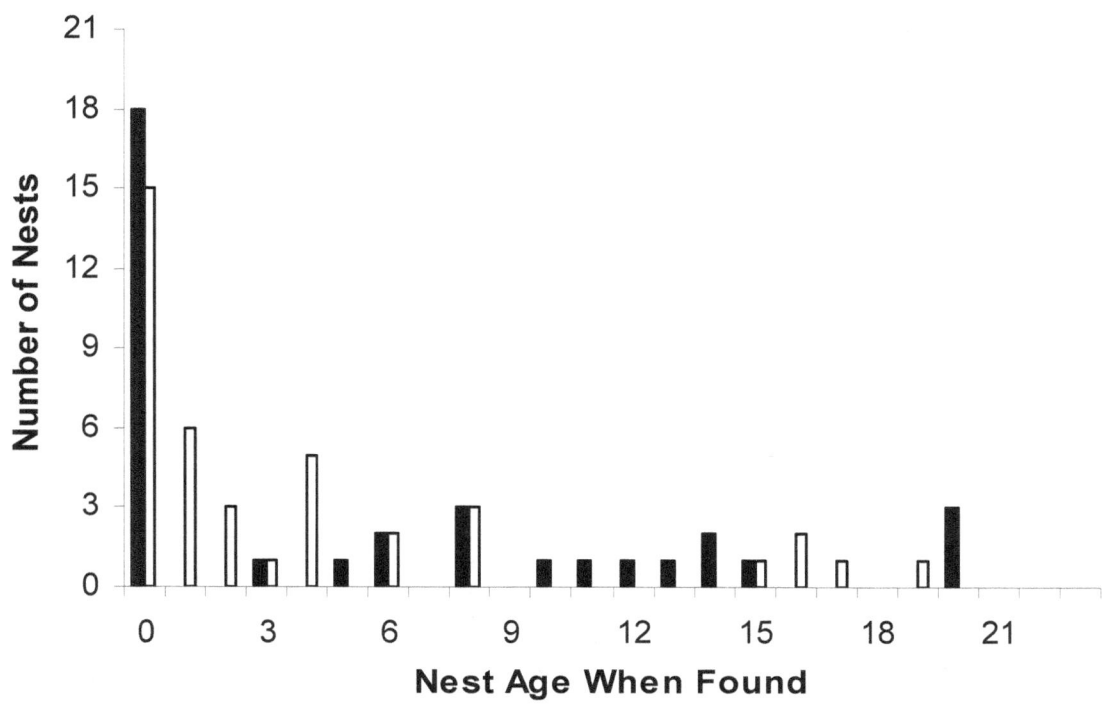

Figure 4. Age of King Eider nests when found in 2003 at Kuparuk (black, n = 39) and Teshekpuk (white, n = 40), Alaska.

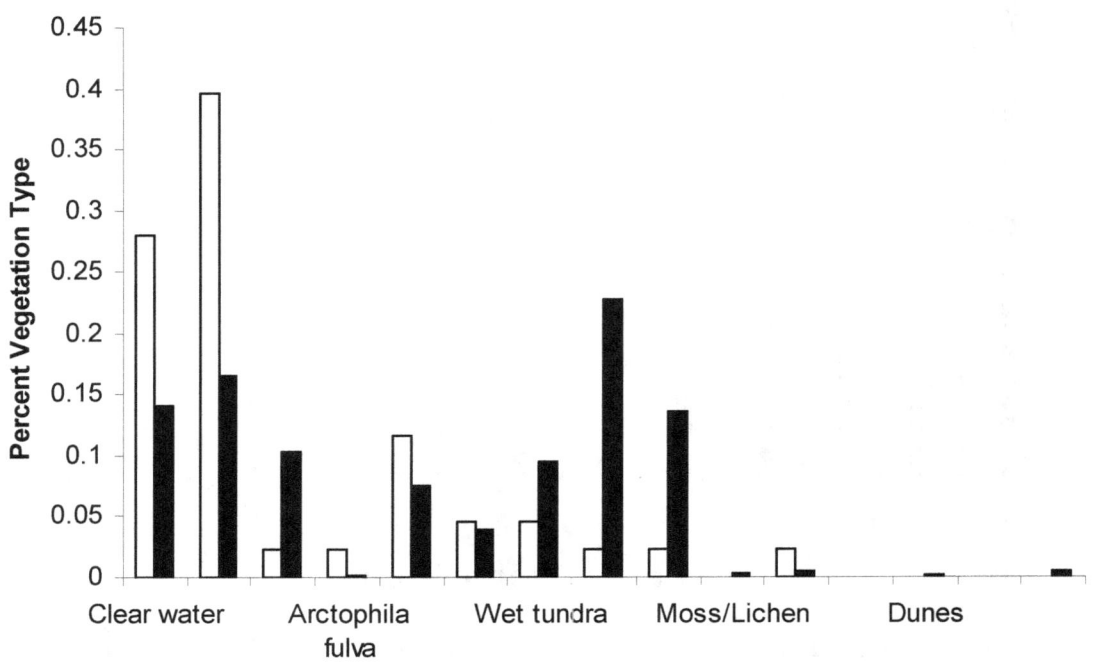

Figure 5. Percent of vegetation types within the entire study area and within 30 m of King Eider nests at Teshekpuk, Alaska, 2002.

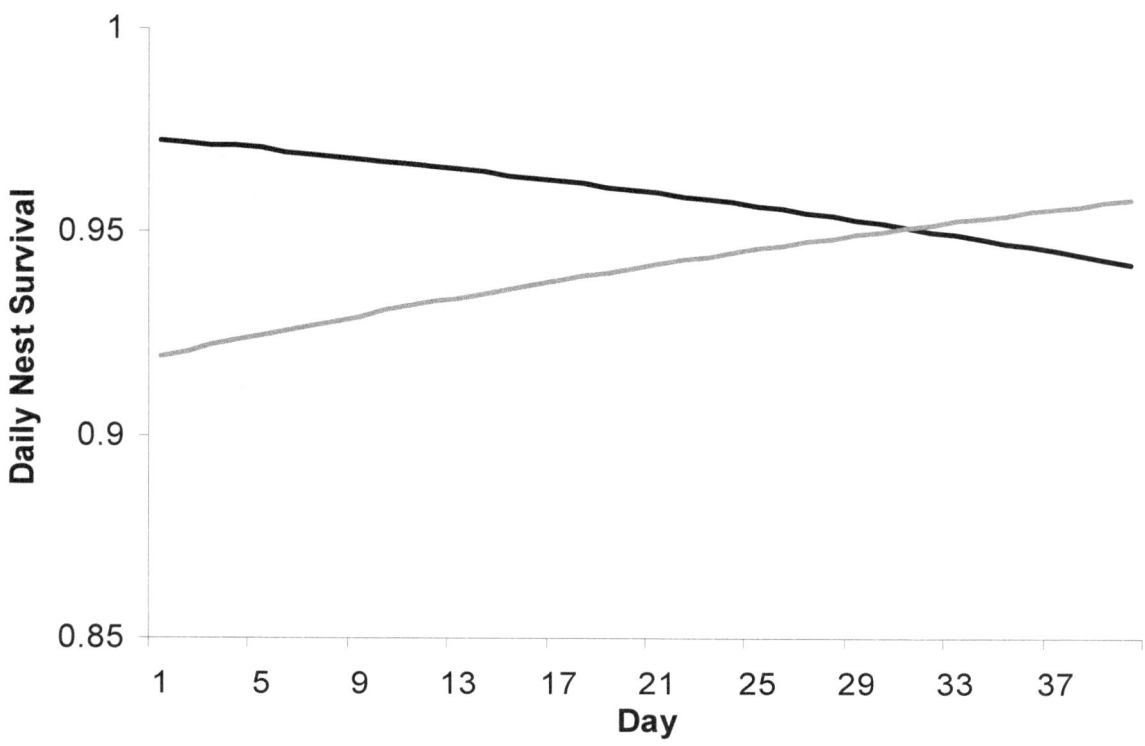

Figure 6. Daily nest survival with a linear trend throughout the season for Teshekpuk (grey line) $B_{T(Teshekpuk)} = 0.02$ (1SE= 0.02, 95% CL = -0.03, 0.06) and Kuparuk (black line) $B_{T(Kuparuk)}= -0.02$ (1SE= 0.02, 95% CL = -0.06, 0.02) for nests on islands ($S_{site*T+island}$).

Table 1. General linear models of nest site selection by King Eiders nesting at Teshekpuk, Alaska, in 2003, with corresponding AIC_c, ΔAIC_c, number of parameters (K), model weight (w_i), and coefficient of determination (r^2). Models are sorted by AIC_c, and those included in the 95% confidence set (sum of w_i =0.95) and the global model are shown. Model parameters of low polygon (LP), low center polygon (LCP), high center polygon (HCP), peninsula, trough, and meadow all refer to the presence of these landforms within 50 m of the nest or random location; length, distance, island, gull and conspecific refer to length of the closest water body, distance to the closest water body, mainland/island location, distance to nearest gull, and distance to the nearest other King Eider, respectively.

Model	K	AIC_c	ΔAIC_c	w_i	r^2
LP, Length, Island, Conspecific	5	82.56	0	0.26	0.38
LP, Peninsula, Length, Island, Gull, Conspecific	7	83.58	1.01	0.16	0.41
LP, LCP, HCP, Peninsula, Length, Island, Gull, Conspecific	9	83.68	1.12	0.15	0.44
LP, HCP, Peninsula, Length, Island, Gull, Conspecific	8	83.96	1.40	0.13	0.42
LP, Length, Island, Gull, Conspecific	6	84.18	1.61	0.12	0.39
LP, HCP, Peninsula, Length, Distance, Island, Gull, Conspecific	9	85.53	2.97	0.06	0.43
LP, LCP, HCP, Peninsula, Length, Distance, Island, Gull, Conspecific	10	85.74	3.18	0.05	0.45
Length, Island, Conspecific	4	87.07	4.51	0.03	0.33
Length, Island, Gull, Conspecific	5	87.92	5.36	0.02	0.34
LP, LCP, HCP, Peninsula, Trough, Distance, Length, Island, Gull, Conspecific	11	87.98	5.42	0.02	0.45
Global	12	90.57	8.01	0.01	0.45

Table 2. Model-averaged parameter estimates (θ), standard errors, and 95% confidence intervals derived from the 95% confidence set of candidate models from the logistic regression analysis of King Eider nest sites and random unoccupied sites at Teshekpuk, Alaska, 2003. See Table 1 for parameter definitions.

Parameter	θ	SE	95% CI
LP	-2.20	1.16	-4.8 to 0.4
LCP	-0.28	0.18	-0.69 to 0.12
HCP	-0.59	0.38	-1.44 to 0.26
Peninsula	0.63	0.43	-0.34 to 1.59
Length	0.00	0.00	-0.00 to 0.00
Distance	0.00	0.00	-0.01 to 0.00
Island	0.96	0.78	-0.77 to 2.7
GLGU	0.08	0.10	-0.13 to 0.3
Conspecific	0.00	0.00	-0.00 to 0.00

Table 3. Factor loadings and eigenvalues from principal components analysis (PCA) of the variable's distance to water, and the percentage of the following vegetation groups within 1 m of the nest or random location: carex, eriophorum, salix, dryas, cassiope, moss, ledum and lichen, Teshekpuk 2003. We interpreted the factor loadings of the principal components with a variance greater than one as the following habitat types; dry tussock tundra dominated by eriophorum, lichen and forbs (tussock), moist tundra dominated by cassiope (moist), dry tundra dominated by cassiope and dryas (dry), dry tundra dominated by salix and carex (dry salix), and moist tundra dominated by salix (moist salix).

	Tussock	Moist	Dry	Dry salix	Moist salix
Distance to water	0.26	-0.56	0.21	0.19	-0.06
% carex	-0.25	0.13	-0.38	0.48	-0.52
% eriophorum	0.39	-0.57	-0.04	0.08	0.01
% salix	-0.19	0.08	-0.02	0.32	0.83
% dryas	0.19	0.29	0.59	0.18	-0.11
% cassiope	0.32	0.35	0.41	-0.01	-0.09
% moss	-0.32	-0.12	0.11	-0.73	-0.06
% ledum	0.44	0.15	-0.47	-0.20	0.08
% lichen	0.49	0.29	-0.27	-0.14	0.08
Eigenvalue	2.12	1.42	1.35	1.21	1.07

Table 4. General linear models of nest site selection by King Eiders at the 1 m scale, with corresponding AIC_c, ΔAIC_c, , number of parameters (K), model weight (w_i), and coefficient of determination (r^2), Teshekpuk, Alaska, 2003. Models are sorted by AIC_c and all candidate models are shown. Model parameters include tussock, moist, dry, dry salix, and moist salix habitat types.

Model	K	AIC_c	ΔAIC_c	w_i	r^2
Tussock, Moist, Dry salix, Moist salix	5	97.71	0.00	0.71	0.33
Tussock, Moist, Dry, Dry salix, Moist salix					
(Global model)	6	100.01	2.29	0.22	0.33
Tussock, Dry salix, Moist salix	4	103.46	5.75	0.04	0.27
Tussock, Moist salix	3	103.96	6.24	0.03	0.25
Tussock	2	113.30	15.59	0.00	0.15
Moist salix	2	116.58	18.87	0.00	0.12
Dry salix	2	124.79	27.08	0.00	0.02
Moist salix	2	125.89	28.17	0.00	0.02
Dry	2	127.34	29.63	0.00	0.01

Table 5. Model-averaged parameter estimates (θ), standard errors and 95% confidence intervals derived from the 99% confidence set of candidate models from the logistic regression analysis of King Eider nest sites and random unoccupied sites at the 1 m scale at Teshekpuk, Alaska, 2003. See Table 3 for parameter definitions.

Parameter	θ	SE	95% CI
Tussock	-1.09	0.37	-1.91 to -0.28
Moist	1.18	0.51	0.04 to 2.32
Dry	0.00	0.07	-0.15 to 0.16
Dry Salix	-0.62	0.28	-1.26 to 0.01
Moist Salix	0.98	0.34	0.22 to 1.73

Table 6. General linear models of nest site selection by King Eiders nesting at Kuparuk, Alaska, in 2003, with corresponding AIC_c, ΔAIC_c, number of parameters (K), model weight (w_i), and coefficient of determination (r^2). Models are sorted by AIC_c, and those included in the 92% confidence set (sum of w_i =0.92) and the global model are shown. Model parameters of low polygon (LP), low center polygon (LCP), high center polygon (HCP), strangmoor, peninsula, trough, and meadow all refer to the presence of these landforms within 50 m of the nest or random location; length, distance, island, gull, and conspecific refer to length of the closest water body, distance to the closest water body, mainland/island location, distance to nearest gull and distance to the nearest other King Eider, respectively.

Model	K	AIC_c	ΔAIC_c	w_i	r^2
HCP, Peninsula, Trough, Distance, Gull, Conspecific	7	57.16	0.00	0.22	0.53
HCP, Peninsula, Trough, Island, Distance, Gull, Conspecific	8	57.50	0.35	0.18	0.55
LP, LCP, HCP, Strangmoor, Peninsula, Trough, Distance, Island, Gull, Conspecific	11	57.72	0.56	0.17	0.60
Trough, Distance, Gull, Conspecific	5	57.76	0.60	0.16	0.49
HCP, Strangmoor, Peninsula, Trough, Distance, Island, Gull, Conspecific	9	58.36	1.20	0.12	0.56
Peninsula, Trough, Distance, Gull, Conspecific	6	59.26	2.11	0.08	0.50
Global	12	60.48	3.33	0.04	0.60

Table 7. Model-averaged parameter estimates (θ), standard errors, and 95% confidence intervals derived from the 92% confidence set of candidate models from the logistic regression analysis of King Eider nest sites and random unoccupied sites at Kuparuk, Alaska, 2003. See Table 6 for parameter definitions.

Parameter	θ	SE	95% CI
LP	0.22	0.65	-0.1 to 1.27
LCP	0.58	0.31	-1.23 to 1.67
HCP	-1.79	1.15	-4.36 to 0.78
Strangemoor	-0.47	0.41	-1.39 to 0.44
Peninsula	0.86	0.99	-1.36 to 3.09
Trough	-3.57	1.49	-6.9 to -0.23
Distance	-0.05	0.05	-0.15 to 0.05
Island	0.70	0.48	-0.38 to 1.78
GLGU	0.00	0.01	-0.01 to 0.02
Conspecific	0.00	0.01	-0.01 to 0.02

Table 8. Factor loadings and eigenvalues from principal components analysis (PCA) of the variable's distance to water, and the percentage of the following vegetation groups within 1 m of the nest or random location: carex, eriophorum, salix, dryas, cassiope, moss, ledum and lichen, Kuparuk 2003. We interpreted the factor loadings as the following habitat types; dry tundra dominated by ledum and lichen (dry), dry tundra dominated by salix and moss (dry salix), moist tundra dominated by salix and dryas (moist salix), moist tundra dominated by carex (carex meadow), and moist forb dominated tundra (moist forb).

	Dry	Dry salix	Moist salix	Carex meadow	Moist forb
Distance to water	0.53	0.22	0.18	-0.02	-0.19
% carex	-0.17	-0.01	0.00	0.78	-0.02
% eriophorum	0.07	-0.23	-0.42	-0.23	-0.61
% salix	-0.13	0.42	0.48	-0.44	-0.06
% dryas	0.03	-0.51	0.55	-0.01	0.26
% cassiope	0.14	-0.18	-0.45	-0.31	0.62
% moss	-0.10	0.63	-0.22	0.10	0.31
% ledum	0.57	0.17	-0.01	0.17	-0.05
% lichen	0.56	-0.08	0.04	0.10	0.17
Eigenvalue	2.54	1.26	1.21	1.16	1.04

Table 9. General linear models of nest site selection by King Eiders at the 1 m scale, with corresponding AIC_c, ΔAIC_c, , number of parameters (K), model weight (w_i), and coefficient of determination (r^2), Kuparuk, Alaska, 2003. Models are sorted by AIC_c and those included in the 99% confidence set (sum of w_i=0.99) are shown. Model parameters include dry, dry salix, moist salix, carex meadow, and moist forb habitat types.

Model	K	AIC_c	ΔAIC_c	w_i	r^2
Dry, Dry salix, Moist salix, Carex meadow,	5	53.56	0.00	0.48	0.44
Dry, Moist salix, Carex meadow,	4	53.85	0.29	0.41	0.43
Dry, Carex meadow	3	57.70	4.14	0.06	0.40
Dry	2	58.05	4.49	0.05	0.40
Dry, Dry salix, Moist salix, Carex meadow, Moist forb (Global)	6	66.89	13.33	0.00	0.44

Table 10. Model-averaged parameter estimates (θ), standard errors, and 95% confidence intervals derived from the 99% confidence set of candidate models from the logistic regression analysis of King Eider nest sites and random unoccupied sites at the 1 m scale at Kuparuk, Alaska, 2003. See Table 8 for parameter definitions.

Parameter	θ	SE	95% CI
Dry	-3.57	1.20	-6.26 to -0.89
Dry Salix	-0.11	0.20	-0.55 to 0.34
Moist salix	-0.62	0.34	-1.37 to 0.13
Carex Meadow	0.13	0.38	-0.72 to 0.98

Table 11. Summary of model selection results for the nest survival of King Eiders at two sites on the North Slope of Alaska, Teshekpuk and Kuparuk, in 2002 and 2003. Models are ranked by ascending ΔAIC_c; w_i is the model weight and K is the number of parameters. Factors in the top models included year, site, island/mainland nest location, a linear time trend (T), a quadratic time trend (TT), and distance to the nearest conspecific (conspecific).

Model	Deviance	K	AIC_c	ΔAIC_c	w_i
$S_{site+island}$	507.73	3	513.82	0	0.51
$S_{site*T+island}$	506.23	5	516.45	2.63	0.14
$S_{site*TT+island}$	504.41	6	516.73	2.90	0.12
$S_{site*conspecific+island}$	506.63	5	516.85	3.03	0.11
$S_{site*conspecific}$	514.56	2	518.60	5.12	0.04
$S_{site*T*conspecific+island}$	505.13	7	519.56	5.73	0.03

Table 12. Estimates of nest survival over a 27-day interval (23-day incubation + 4 day average laying period) from the best approximating model ($S_{site+island}$) for King Eiders at Teshekpuk and Kuparuk, in 2002 and 2003.

	Mainland (Mean ± SE)	Islands (Mean ± SE)
Kuparuk	0.14 ± 0.05	0.36 ± 0.07
Teshekpuk	0.04 ± 0.02	0.17 ± 0.48

www.ingramcontent.com/pod-product-compliance
Lightning Source LLC
Chambersburg PA
CBHW080928290526
45795CB00007BA/2680